"The Most Effective Adapt Your YouTube Channel,"

Introduction :

Welcome to "The Most Effective Method to Adapt Your YouTube Channel," an essential guide designed to empower content creators in navigating the intricate landscape of YouTube earnings. In this eBook, we embark on an insightful journey, uncovering the diverse avenues available to transform your passion for creating videos into a lucrative venture.

YouTube has evolved beyond a mere platform for sharing videos; it's a bustling marketplace teeming with opportunities for those who understand its nuances. From mastering the art of engaging content creation to deciphering the intricate algorithms governing visibility and growth, this guide provides a comprehensive roadmap.

Discover the strategic significance of subscriber count, engagement metrics, and niche targeting to attract both viewership and potential sponsors. Explore the multifaceted realm of monetization options, including advertising revenue, brand partnerships, merchandise sales, and the lucrative realm of affiliate marketing.

Moreover, we delve into the importance of building a strong personal brand, fostering audience loyalty, and harnessing the power of analytics to make informed decisions that elevate your channel's financial prospects.

Whether you're an aspiring YouTuber or seeking to optimize your existing channel's revenue streams, "The Most Effective Method to Adapt Your YouTube Channel," equips you with actionable insights and proven strategies to monetize your content effectively. Get ready to embark on a transformative journey towards turning your passion into a sustainable source of income on YouTube.

INDEX

Here are 15 effective ways to "The Most Effective Method to Adapt Your YouTube Channel,":

1. **Advertising Revenue:** Utilize Google AdSense to earn money through ads displayed on your videos.

2. **Affiliate Marketing:** Promote products or services in your videos with affiliate links to earn commissions on sales.

3. **Sponsorships and Brand Deals:** Collaborate with brands or sponsors for sponsored content or product placements.

4. **Channel Memberships:** Offer exclusive perks or content to subscribers who become channel members for a recurring fee.

5. **Merchandise Sales:** Create and sell branded merchandise (e.g., clothing, accessories) related to your channel.

6. **Crowdfunding:** Use platforms like Patreon or Kickstarter to receive financial support from your audience.

7. **Super Chat and Super Stickers:** Enable viewers to purchase highlighted messages or stickers during live streams.

8. **YouTube Premium Revenue:** Earn a share of the subscription fees paid by YouTube Premium users who watch your content.

9. **Fan Funding:** Enable viewers to donate directly to support your channel through platforms like PayPal or Venmo.

10. **Online Courses or Workshops:** Share your expertise by offering paid courses or workshops related to your channel's niche.

11. **Consulting or Coaching Services:** Provide personalized services or consultations based on your expertise.

12. **Live Events and Meet-ups:** Organize paid live events, workshops, or meet-ups for your audience.

13. **Selling Digital Products:** Offer digital downloads such as eBooks, presets, or templates related to your content.

14. **Licensing Content:** License your videos or footage to media outlets, agencies, or businesses.

15. **Subscription-based Content:** Create a subscription model for exclusive content, behind-the-scenes access, or special features.

Each of these strategies presents an opportunity to diversify your revenue streams and maximize your earnings potential as a YouTube content creator. Experimenting with a combination of these methods tailored to your channel's niche and audience can significantly boost your overall monetization efforts.

Chapter- 1

1. **Advertising Revenue:** Utilize Google AdSense to earn money through ads displayed on your videos.

Utilizing Google AdSense to earn revenue through ads displayed on your YouTube videos is a fundamental aspect of monetizing your channel. This method allows content creators to tap into the vast advertising network of Google and generate income based on ad impressions and clicks.

Google AdSense serves as the intermediary between advertisers and content creators, facilitating the placement of relevant ads within videos. For YouTube creators, the process begins by meeting specific eligibility criteria set by YouTube, including adhering to the platform's monetization policies, having an active AdSense account, and amassing a minimum threshold of 1,000 subscribers and 4,000 watch hours within the last 12 months.

Once these prerequisites are met, creators can apply for YouTube's Partner Program, which enables them to monetize their videos by enabling advertisements. Upon acceptance, creators gain access to the YouTube Studio dashboard, where they can manage their monetization settings and choose the types of ads to display within their content.

Ad formats available for YouTube videos include display ads, overlay ads, skippable and non-skippable video ads, and sponsored cards. Each format offers distinct advantages, such as viewer engagement or higher revenue potential, and creators can opt to enable specific ad formats based on their preferences and audience experience.

Google AdSense employs a revenue-sharing model, where creators typically receive a portion of the advertising revenue generated from their videos. The actual earnings vary based on several factors, including ad engagement, viewer demographics, ad quality, and the overall performance of the channel.

Creators can track their ad revenue and performance metrics through the YouTube Analytics dashboard, providing valuable insights into which videos generate the most revenue, viewer engagement with ads, and demographic information of their audience.

To optimize earnings through AdSense, creators often focus on enhancing video content quality, increasing viewer engagement, and optimizing video length and format to accommodate ads effectively without compromising user experience. Strategies such as improving watch time, encouraging longer viewer sessions, and creating compelling content can indirectly impact ad revenue by attracting more advertisers and higher-paying ads.

However, it's crucial to strike a balance between ad monetization and viewer satisfaction. Excessive or intrusive ads may lead to a negative viewer experience, potentially reducing audience retention and engagement. Hence, creators often experiment with ad placements and formats to find the optimal balance that maximizes revenue while maintaining a positive viewer experience.

Moreover, creators need to remain vigilant about adhering to YouTube's community guidelines and ad policies to prevent potential demonetization or penalties that could impact their revenue stream. Violations, such as inappropriate content, copyright infringement, or engagement in fraudulent practices, could lead to demonetization or suspension of ad serving on specific videos or the entire channel.

In conclusion, Google AdSense offers YouTube creators a powerful avenue to monetize their content by leveraging the platform's extensive advertising network. When utilized effectively, AdSense can be a significant revenue stream, providing creators with the opportunity to turn their passion for creating videos into a sustainable source of income. However, achieving success with ad monetization requires a strategic approach, continuous content improvement, adherence to policies, and a focus on delivering quality content that resonates with the audience while incorporating ads seamlessly into the viewing experience.

Chapter- 2

2. **Affiliate Marketing:** Promote products or services in your videos with affiliate links to earn commissions on sales

Affiliate marketing on YouTube presents an influential way for content creators to earn revenue by promoting products or services through unique affiliate links within their videos. This strategy allows creators to partner with brands or affiliate programs, earning commissions for every sale or action generated through their referral.

The process begins with creators establishing partnerships with suitable affiliate programs or directly with brands that align with their channel's niche and audience interests. Joining an affiliate program typically involves registering with the respective platform, agreeing to its terms, and gaining access to unique affiliate links or promotional codes.

Once affiliated, creators integrate these affiliate links seamlessly into their video content, often in the video description or through direct mentions or endorsements during the video. These links direct viewers to the product or service being promoted, and when viewers make a purchase or take a specified action through these links, the creator earns a commission or predetermined reward.

The success of affiliate marketing on YouTube hinges on various factors, including audience trust, content relevance, and the authenticity of the creator's recommendations. Authenticity plays a pivotal role as viewers value genuine endorsements from creators they trust. Therefore, creators often review or showcase products/services they genuinely believe in, ensuring transparency about their affiliation and maintaining credibility with their audience.

Strategically incorporating affiliate promotions into content without appearing overly promotional or disruptive is crucial. Creators often blend these promotions naturally within their videos, providing valuable information, tutorials, or demonstrations related to the promoted product/service, thereby enhancing the viewer's understanding and interest in the offering.

Choosing the right products/services to promote is equally vital. Content creators typically opt for items that resonate with their audience's interests, solve specific problems, or enhance their lifestyle in some way. Aligning the promoted offerings with the audience's needs and preferences increases the likelihood of conversions and successful affiliate earnings.

To measure the performance of affiliate marketing efforts, creators often track metrics such as click-through rates, conversion rates, and overall revenue generated through their affiliate links. Utilizing affiliate dashboards or analytics provided by affiliate programs offers insights into the effectiveness of different promotional strategies and helps optimize future campaigns.

Creators need to comply with disclosure guidelines and regulations regarding affiliate marketing. This includes disclosing their affiliate relationships to their audience, either verbally within the video or prominently in the video description, ensuring transparency and honesty about their financial incentives.

Maintaining a balance between providing valuable content and integrating affiliate promotions tastefully is key. Overuse of affiliate links or overly aggressive promotional tactics may lead to a negative viewer experience and affect audience trust and engagement adversely.

In conclusion, affiliate marketing stands as a lucrative monetization strategy for YouTube creators, offering a way to earn income while providing valuable content to their audience. Successful affiliate marketing relies on authenticity, relevance, and audience trust, emphasizing the importance of genuine recommendations and seamless integration of affiliate links within engaging and informative content. By fostering genuine connections with their audience and selecting appropriate affiliate partnerships, content creators can leverage affiliate marketing to augment their revenue streams and enhance their overall content strategy on YouTube.

Chapter- 3

3. **Sponsorships and Brand Deals:** Collaborate with brands or sponsors for sponsored content or product placements.

Collaborating with brands or sponsors for sponsored content or product placements is a prominent monetization avenue for YouTube content creators. It involves forming partnerships with brands to promote their products or services within the content in exchange for compensation, free products, or other mutually agreed-upon benefits.

The process of securing sponsorships typically begins with creators establishing a strong and engaged audience base on their YouTube channel. Brands often seek creators whose audience demographics align with their target market. As a result, content creators with a niche audience or a substantial following are more likely to attract sponsorship opportunities.

Content creators can explore sponsorship opportunities through various channels, including direct outreach to brands, joining influencer marketing platforms, or partnering with agencies specializing in connecting creators with brands seeking promotion.

Negotiating sponsorship deals involves discussions on the scope of collaboration, deliverables, compensation, and adherence to FTC guidelines and disclosure regulations. These discussions often include the format of sponsored content, such as dedicated product reviews, integration of products within videos, or endorsement through shoutouts or mentions.

Once a sponsorship agreement is established, creators integrate the sponsored content organically into their videos, ensuring it aligns with their audience's interests and fits seamlessly into the overall narrative of the video. Authenticity is crucial, and creators strive to provide genuine and valuable insights about the sponsored products or services to maintain trust with their audience.

Brands may provide creators with specific guidelines or talking points to ensure that the sponsored content meets their marketing objectives and aligns with their brand image. However, content creators often have creative freedom to present the sponsored offerings in a way that resonates best with their audience.

Disclosure is a key aspect of sponsored content. Creators are required by FTC guidelines to disclose their relationship with the brand or sponsor to their audience. This transparency builds trust and ensures that viewers are aware of any potential bias or financial incentives behind the promotion.

Measuring the success of sponsored content involves analyzing various metrics, including engagement rates, click-through rates on affiliate links or promo codes, and overall brand visibility. This data helps both creators and brands evaluate the effectiveness of the collaboration and refine future strategies.

Successful sponsorships not only benefit creators financially but also offer opportunities for audience engagement and exposure to new products or services. However, creators must strike a balance between sponsored and non-sponsored content to maintain the integrity of their channel and prevent viewer fatigue from excessive promotions.

In conclusion, sponsorships and brand deals represent a mutually beneficial arrangement for both content creators and brands. For creators, these collaborations offer a way to monetize their content while providing valuable exposure to brands. When executed authentically and transparently, sponsored content can enhance the viewer experience, strengthen audience engagement, and contribute significantly to a creator's revenue stream on YouTube. The key lies in fostering meaningful partnerships, delivering genuine endorsements, and maintaining the trust and interest of the audience.

Chapter- 4

4. **Channel Memberships:** Offer exclusive perks or content to subscribers who become channel members for a recurring fee.

Channel Memberships on YouTube provide creators with an opportunity to offer exclusive perks or content to subscribers who opt to become paying members, contributing a recurring fee to support the channel. This feature allows content creators to foster a sense of community among their audience while generating a consistent source of revenue.

To initiate Channel Memberships, creators need to meet specific eligibility criteria set by YouTube, such as having at least 30,000 subscribers, adhering to the platform's monetization policies, and being located in an eligible country where Memberships are available.

Once eligible, creators can enable Channel Memberships through the YouTube Partner Program. This feature allows creators to create multiple tiers or levels of membership, each offering distinct perks or benefits to subscribers who choose to support the channel by becoming members.

The perks offered to Channel Members often include exclusive badges or emojis that members can use in live chats or comments, access to members-only community posts, special shoutouts, behind-the-scenes content, exclusive live streams, early access to videos, customised merchandise or discounts, and direct interaction or Q&A sessions with the creator.

Creators can customize the perks offered in each membership tier, providing different levels of benefits corresponding to varying subscription price points. For instance, higher-tier members may receive more exclusive perks or access to premium content compared to lower-tier members.

To encourage viewers to become channel members, creators often highlight the benefits of membership in their videos, live streams, or through dedicated posts on their channels. They may also create compelling promotional content or exclusive previews to entice non-members to join and access the exclusive perks.

The revenue generated through Channel Memberships is split between the creator and YouTube, with creators receiving a significant portion of the membership fees paid by subscribers. The revenue share varies based on the creator's agreement with YouTube and the country's policies where the channel is located.

Monitoring the performance of Channel Memberships involves tracking metrics such as the number of members in each tier, subscription retention rates, and engagement with exclusive content. Creators utilize YouTube Analytics to assess the impact of Memberships on their channel's overall growth and revenue.

Maintaining active engagement and fostering a sense of community among channel members is crucial. Creators often interact directly with members through exclusive posts, live streams, or dedicated community sections, making them feel valued and appreciated for their support.

Consistency in delivering exclusive content and perks is essential to retain members and attract new subscribers. Creators continually strive to offer fresh and appealing content to incentivize viewers to become members and sustain their membership over time.

Transparency in communicating the value of Channel Memberships and the benefits offered is pivotal. Creators frequently outline the perks available at different membership levels, ensuring that potential members understand what they will receive in exchange for their support.

However, it's crucial to strike a balance between promoting Channel Memberships and maintaining the core focus on providing high-quality, accessible content for all viewers. Exclusivity should enhance the viewer experience without alienating non-members.

In conclusion, Channel Memberships on YouTube serve as a valuable means for creators to monetize their content while establishing a closer connection with their audience. By offering exclusive perks and content, creators can create a dedicated community of supporters willing to contribute financially to sustain the channel. When managed effectively, Channel Memberships can significantly enhance a creator's revenue stream, nurture audience engagement, and fortify the channel's long-term sustainability on the platform.

Chapter- 5

5. **Merchandise Sales:** Create and sell branded merchandise (e.g., clothing, accessories) related to your channel.

Leveraging merchandise sales on YouTube involves creating and selling branded products, including clothing, accessories, or other items that resonate with the channel's theme or content. This strategy empowers content creators to expand their revenue streams while offering their audience tangible items that represent their brand and content.

To embark on merchandise sales, creators typically partner with merchandising platforms or companies that facilitate the creation, production, and distribution of branded items. These platforms offer a range of customizable products, such as t-shirts, hoodies, hats, mugs, stickers, or unique items related to the channel's niche.

The process begins with designing the merchandise. Creators often collaborate with graphic designers or use their creativity to develop compelling and unique designs that reflect their brand identity and resonate with their audience. These designs could feature logos, catchphrases, artwork, or imagery closely associated with the channel.

Once the designs are finalized, creators upload them to the merchandising platform's interface, where they can select the types of products to offer, customize product variations (e.g., colours, sizes), set prices, and create storefronts or dedicated sections on their channel to showcase the merchandise.

Promotion is pivotal in driving merchandise sales. Creators leverage various strategies to market their merchandise, including featuring the products in their videos, creating dedicated merch announcement videos, incorporating product placements, or showcasing the items during live streams. Additionally, they often use social media, community posts, and email newsletters to reach a broader audience and generate interest in their branded merchandise.

Engaging with the audience and soliciting their input can also be beneficial. Conducting polls or surveys to gauge interest in specific designs or types of merchandise allows creators to tailor their offerings to meet their audience's preferences, thus increasing the likelihood of sales.

Transparency and authenticity are crucial in promoting merchandise. Creators emphasize the quality and uniqueness of their products, highlighting the value they bring to their audience. Building a narrative around the merchandise, sharing stories or reasons behind the designs, and showcasing the products in use can resonate well with viewers and drive sales.

Managing inventory and fulfilment logistics are handled by the merchandising platform or third-party companies, relieving creators of the burden of handling product manufacturing, storage, and shipping. This allows creators to focus on content creation while the platform manages the production and delivery of orders to customers.

Monitoring sales performance and tracking key metrics such as sales volume, popular products, and customer feedback is essential. This data aids creators in evaluating the success of their merchandise line, identifying popular designs, and making informed decisions for future product launches or adjustments.

Ensuring customer satisfaction is paramount. Creators aim to deliver quality products and exceptional customer service to maintain a positive brand image and encourage repeat purchases. Addressing customer inquiries, handling returns or exchanges promptly, and seeking feedback for continuous improvement are integral aspects of successful merchandise sales.

However, creators must strike a balance between promoting merchandise and preserving the primary focus on content creation. Excessive or overly aggressive promotion may deter viewers, impacting their viewing experience and diminishing engagement.

In conclusion, merchandise sales present a lucrative opportunity for YouTube creators to diversify their revenue streams while offering their audience tangible products that embody their brand. By partnering with merchandising platforms, creating compelling designs, and implementing effective promotional strategies, creators can harness the power of branded merchandise to enhance their channel's financial sustainability, strengthen audience engagement, and forge a deeper connection with their community of supporters. When executed thoughtfully, merchandise sales can serve as a valuable and complementary aspect of a creator's YouTube channel monetization strategy.

Chapter - 6

6. **Crowdfunding:** Use platforms like Patreon or Kickstarter to receive financial support from your audience.

Crowdfunding through platforms like Patreon or Kickstarter offers content creators on YouTube a powerful means to receive financial support directly from their audience. This method allows creators to build a community of dedicated patrons or backers who contribute funds to support their ongoing content creation efforts.

Patreon stands as a popular crowdfunding platform where creators can set up membership tiers, offering exclusive perks or rewards to patrons in exchange for their financial support. Kickstarter, on the other hand, is primarily used for launching specific projects or campaigns, allowing creators to set funding goals and offer rewards to backers.

Creators often opt for Patreon due to its subscription-based model, enabling patrons to pledge a recurring monthly payment to support the creator. These pledges are often tiered, offering various benefits or exclusive content to patrons based on their level of support. These perks may include access to behind-the-scenes content, exclusive live streams, early access to videos, merchandise discounts, or direct interaction with the creator.

The process of establishing a Patreon account involves creators setting up their page, outlining the different membership tiers and corresponding benefits, and promoting the Patreon page across their YouTube channel, social media, and other platforms. Creators then encourage their audience to become patrons and support their work by joining the Patreon community.

Kickstarter, on the other hand, operates on a project-based funding model, where creators set a funding goal and a timeframe to reach that goal. Backers contribute funds towards the project, and creators offer rewards or incentives based on the backers' pledge amounts. This platform is often used for launching new creative projects, such as producing a film, creating a book, or developing a new product or service.

Promotion plays a pivotal role in crowdfunding success. Creators leverage their YouTube channel, social media presence, and email newsletters to create awareness about their Patreon or Kickstarter campaigns. They often create dedicated videos or promotional content to explain the benefits of supporting their work and encourage viewers to become patrons or backers.

Building and maintaining engagement with patrons or backers is crucial. Creators regularly communicate with their supporters, providing updates, exclusive content, or personalized messages to foster a sense of community and gratitude for their support. Interaction through live Q&A sessions, private Discord channels, or patron-only events further strengthens the bond between creators and their supporters.

Moreover, creators continually strive to deliver on their promises and provide value to their patrons or backers. Fulfilling rewards, offering exclusive content, and ensuring a positive and rewarding experience for supporters are vital aspects of sustaining a successful crowdfunding campaign.

Monitoring the performance of crowdfunding efforts involves tracking metrics such as the number of patrons/backers, pledge amounts, funding goals reached, and overall engagement. This data aids creators in evaluating the effectiveness of their campaigns, refining their strategies, and adapting to their audience's preferences.

Transparency in communicating goals, progress, and how the funds will be utilized is essential. Creators often provide detailed information about how the funds will support their content creation efforts, ensuring transparency and trust with their audience.

However, it's essential to strike a balance between promoting crowdfunding campaigns and maintaining the primary focus on creating high-quality content. Overly aggressive promotion may alienate viewers and impact their viewing experience negatively.

 In conclusion, crowdfunding platforms like Patreon and Kickstarter offer content creators on YouTube an avenue to receive direct financial support from their audience. By leveraging these platforms, creators can build a dedicated community of supporters willing to contribute financially to sustain their content creation efforts. When executed effectively, crowdfunding not only provides financial backing but also fosters a closer connection between creators and their audience, enabling creators to pursue their creative endeavours and build sustainable careers on YouTube.

Chapter- 7

7. **Super Chat and Super Stickers:** Enable viewers to purchase highlighted messages or stickers during live streams.

Super Chat and Super Stickers feature on YouTube enables viewers to purchase highlighted messages or animated stickers during live streams, allowing them to engage more prominently with content creators and stand out in the live chat. These features provide a way for viewers to support their favourite creators monetarily while gaining increased visibility and interaction during live-streaming sessions.

Super Chat allows viewers to purchase highlighted messages that appear prominently in the live chat stream during a creator's live broadcast. These messages are often highlighted in different colours, pinned for a specified duration, and sometimes accompanied by an animated effect, depending on the amount paid by the viewer. This feature enables viewers to make their messages more visible to the creator and other viewers watching the livestream.

Super Stickers, on the other hand, are animated stickers or emojis that viewers can purchase and send during live streams as a form of support or to express their reactions to the content. These stickers come in various designs, animations, and sizes, offering viewers a visually engaging way to interact with the live stream and convey their emotions or sentiments to the creator and the live chat audience.

To access Super Chat and Super Stickers during live streams, viewers can click on the dollar sign icon within the live chat window, which prompts them to choose the amount they wish to pay for their message or sticker. The more significant the contribution, the longer the message stays highlighted or the more elaborate the sticker animation.

For creators, enabling Super Chat and Super Stickers requires participation in the YouTube Partner Program and having an active monetized channel. Once these criteria are met, creators can enable these features in their live stream settings, allowing viewers to purchase Super Chats or Super Stickers during their live broadcasts.

During live streams, creators often encourage their audience to use Super Chat and Super Stickers by explaining the features, expressing gratitude for contributions, and offering shoutouts or acknowledgements to viewers who make purchases. Creators may also set goals or challenges tied to Super Chat or Super Sticker contributions, adding an interactive element to the live stream and motivating viewers to participate.

The revenue generated through Super Chat and Super Stickers is split between the creator and YouTube, with creators receiving a portion of the amount paid by viewers. The revenue share varies based on the viewer's country and the currency used for the purchase.

Monitoring the performance of Super Chat and Super Stickers involves tracking metrics such as the number of Super Chats or Stickers received, the total revenue generated, and the engagement levels during live streams. Creators can access this data through YouTube Analytics, providing insights into the effectiveness of these features and their impact on viewer engagement.

Maintaining a balance between encouraging Super Chats and Stickers and ensuring a quality viewing experience is crucial. Creators strive to foster a supportive and engaging environment for their audience without overshadowing the primary content of the livestream.

In conclusion, Super Chat and Super Stickers on YouTube offer viewers a means to financially support content creators during live streams while gaining increased visibility and interaction within the live chat. These features provide a way for viewers to express their appreciation for the creator's content and enhance their participation in the live-streaming experience. For creators, Super Chat and Super Stickers represent an additional revenue stream and a means to engage more intimately with their audience during live broadcasts. When used effectively, these features contribute to fostering a more vibrant and supportive community around a creator's content on YouTube.

Chapter- 8

8. **YouTube Premium Revenue:** Earn a share of the subscription fees paid by YouTube Premium users who watch your content.

 YouTube Premium Revenue is a monetization avenue available to content creators, enabling them to earn a share of the subscription fees paid by YouTube Premium users who watch their content. YouTube Premium is a subscription-based service offered by YouTube, providing users with an ad-free viewing experience, offline playback, access to YouTube Originals, and other premium features.

YouTube Premium subscribers pay a monthly subscription fee to access these benefits, and a portion of that subscription revenue is allocated to creators based on various factors, including watch time from Premium viewers on their content.

Creators participating in the YouTube Partner Program, meeting the necessary eligibility criteria, such as adhering to the platform's monetization policies and having an active AdSense account, are eligible to earn revenue from YouTube Premium viewership.

The revenue share from YouTube Premium is calculated based on a complex algorithm that considers the overall watch time of Premium viewers on a creator's content relative to the total watch time across YouTube. This algorithmic calculation involves a portion of the subscription fees being distributed among creators whose content is watched by Premium subscribers.

YouTube Premium viewership contributes to a creator's overall revenue stream, providing an additional source of income beyond traditional ad-based monetization. However, the exact amount earned from YouTube Premium can vary significantly based on factors such as viewer engagement, watch time, the content's appeal to Premium subscribers, and the overall performance of the channel.

Monitoring the performance and revenue generated from YouTube Premium involves accessing the YouTube Analytics dashboard, which provides insights into the percentage of revenue derived from Premium viewership, watch time metrics, and revenue trends over time. Creators can analyze this data to evaluate the impact of YouTube Premium on their channel's earnings and audience engagement.

As YouTube Premium continues to grow in popularity, creators aim to produce high-quality content that appeals to Premium subscribers, thereby increasing their chances of earning revenue from this source. Premium subscribers often seek content without interruptions from ads, making engaging and ad-free content more appealing to this audience segment.

Maintaining a balance between ad-supported content and content tailored for YouTube Premium viewers is essential. Creators strive to create a diverse range of content that caters to both ad-supported viewers and Premium subscribers while ensuring a seamless and engaging viewing experience for all audiences.

In conclusion, YouTube Premium Revenue offers content creators an opportunity to earn a portion of the subscription fees paid by YouTube Premium users who watch their content. While the specifics of the revenue share are algorithmically determined based on various factors, YouTube Premium represents an additional source of income for creators and incentivizes the production of high-quality, engaging content that appeals to Premium subscribers. As YouTube Premium continues to evolve, creators strive to leverage this monetization avenue by creating content that resonates with both ad-supported viewers and Premium subscribers, thus maximizing their revenue potential on the platform.

Chapter- 9

9. **Fan Funding:** Enable viewers to donate directly to support your channel through platforms like PayPal or Venmo.

Fan Funding, also known as fan donations or direct contributions, allows content creators on platforms like YouTube to receive monetary support directly from their audience through third-party payment platforms such as PayPal, Venmo, Patreon, or other crowdfunding services. This method enables viewers who appreciate a creator's content to voluntarily contribute funds as a gesture of support or appreciation for the content produced.

For content creators, establishing fan funding options often involves integrating payment links or buttons provided by payment platforms into their video descriptions, channel banners, or social media profiles. Creators may also encourage donations during live streams or through dedicated videos that highlight the importance of viewer support in sustaining and improving the channel.

Platforms like PayPal or Venmo offer creators a simple and secure way to receive fan funding, allowing viewers to make one-time or recurring donations. Creators may specify the purpose of donations, such as supporting content creation, improving equipment, funding future projects, or simply showing appreciation for the creator's work.

Fan funding offers creators flexibility in how they utilize the received funds. Whether it's investing in better equipment, enhancing production quality, hiring additional help, or allocating resources to create more diverse and engaging content, the funds collected through fan donations can significantly impact a creator's ability to improve their channel and better serve their audience.

Creators often express gratitude and acknowledge the support received from donors by giving shoutouts, displaying supporter names in video credits, or offering exclusive perks or benefits to donors, such as early access to content, behind-the-scenes updates, or exclusive live streams.

Monitoring fan funding involves tracking contributions received through various payment platforms and analyzing the trends in donation amounts, frequency, and donor engagement. Creators can assess the impact of fan funding on their channel's revenue and audience support, providing insights into the effectiveness of their efforts in encouraging viewer contributions.

Transparency in communicating the purpose of fan funding and how the received funds will be utilized is crucial. Creators often provide updates or progress reports to donors, informing them about how their contributions have positively impacted the channel or supported specific projects.

Maintaining a balance between promoting fan funding and maintaining the primary focus on creating high-quality content is vital. Creators aim to foster a supportive environment for their audience without overshadowing the content itself or pressuring viewers into donating.

In conclusion, fan funding serves as a direct way for viewers to financially support their favourite content creators on platforms like YouTube. Through platforms such as PayPal, Venmo, or Patreon, viewers can contribute funds voluntarily to help creators sustain their channels, improve content quality, and embark on new projects. When utilized thoughtfully, fan funding can significantly complement a creator's revenue streams, foster a stronger connection with their audience, and empower creators to continue producing content that resonates with their supporters.

10. **Online Courses or Workshops:** Share your expertise by offering paid courses or workshops related to your channel's niche.

Offering online courses or workshops related to a channel's niche provides content creators on platforms like YouTube with an opportunity to share their expertise, knowledge, and skills with their audience in a more structured and in-depth format. These paid courses or workshops allow creators to leverage their expertise and provide additional value to their audience while creating an alternate revenue stream.

Creators often possess specialized knowledge or skills within their niche that may not be fully explored or explained in their regular content due to time constraints or the need for more comprehensive explanations. Online courses or workshops serve as a platform for creators to delve deeper into specific topics, offering a structured and comprehensive learning experience for interested viewers.

To initiate online courses or workshops, creators can leverage various platforms or tools specifically designed for course creation, such as Teachable, Udemy, Thinkific, or even their websites. These platforms provide creators with the necessary tools to design, create, and manage their courses, including video lectures, downloadable resources, quizzes, assignments, and discussion forums.

Creators typically identify key topics or areas within their niche that align with their expertise and audience interests to develop course content. The course curriculum is structured to cover these topics systematically, allowing learners to progress from foundational concepts to more advanced or specialized knowledge.

Promotion plays a pivotal role in attracting participants to these courses or workshops. Creators leverage their existing platforms, such as YouTube channels, social media profiles, email newsletters, and websites, to promote their courses or workshops. They may offer sneak peeks, teasers, or introductory content to generate interest and entice their audience to enrol.

Engagement and interaction with course participants are essential components of a successful online course. Creators often incorporate discussion forums, live Q&A sessions, or office hours to provide personalized attention and guidance, fostering a sense of community among learners and encouraging active participation.

Creators aim to provide value beyond what is available for free on their channel, offering in-depth insights, practical advice, case studies, and actionable strategies that learners can apply in real-world scenarios. By delivering high-quality content and ensuring the relevance and applicability of the course material, creators can enhance the learning experience and satisfaction of course participants.

Monitoring the performance of online courses involves tracking metrics such as enrolment numbers, completion rates, learner feedback, and overall satisfaction levels. Creators analyze this data to evaluate the effectiveness of their courses, identify areas for improvement, and refine their future course offerings.

Transparency and credibility in course delivery are crucial. Creators often showcase their credentials, expertise, or testimonials from previous participants to establish trust and credibility among potential learners. This transparency assures learners of the value they will receive from the course and enhances the credibility of the creator as an authority in their niche.

Maintaining a balance between promoting online courses and creating regular content is essential. Creators strive to promote their courses without overwhelming their audience with excessive promotional content, ensuring that their primary focus remains on delivering high-quality free content to their broader audience.

In conclusion, offering online courses or workshops related to a channel's niche presents content creators with an opportunity to share their expertise, provide additional value to their audience, and create an alternative revenue stream. Through structured and comprehensive course content, creators can deepen their connection with their audience, foster a community of learners, and leverage their expertise to empower others within their niche. When executed thoughtfully, online courses can serve as a valuable asset for creators, enabling them to monetize their expertise while contributing positively to their audience's learning and development.

Chapter- 11

11. **Consulting or Coaching Services:** Provide personalized services or consultations based on your expertise.

Offering consulting or coaching services based on one's expertise presents content creators on platforms like YouTube with an opportunity to provide personalized guidance, advice, and support to individuals seeking assistance within their niche. These services allow creators to leverage their knowledge, experience, and skills to offer one-on-one or group consultations, mentoring, or coaching sessions tailored to their clients' specific needs.

Creators often possess specialized knowledge, skills, or experience within their niche that can benefit others seeking guidance, advice, or solutions related to similar areas. Whether it's expertise in fitness, business, personal development, arts, technology, or any other field, creators can offer consulting or coaching services to assist clients in achieving their goals or overcoming challenges.

To initiate consulting or coaching services, creators can establish their services by leveraging various platforms or tools, such as their website, social media profiles, or specialized coaching platforms. They can create service packages outlining the scope, duration, and pricing of their services, along with the benefits and outcomes clients can expect to achieve.

Creators often identify their target audience and the specific problems or needs they aim to address through their consulting or coaching services. This helps in tailoring their services to meet the requirements of their clients effectively.

Promotion and marketing play a vital role in attracting clients to these services. Creators leverage their existing platforms, such as YouTube channels, social media, email newsletters, and websites, to promote their consulting or coaching services. They may offer free resources, conduct webinars, or share success stories to showcase the value and expertise they bring to potential clients.

Engagement and interaction with clients are key aspects of consulting or coaching services. Creators aim to build strong relationships with their clients, understanding their unique needs, providing personalised advice, and offering practical strategies or solutions that clients can implement to achieve their objectives.

Creators ensure the credibility and effectiveness of their services by highlighting their credentials, experience, success stories, client testimonials, or case studies. This establishes trust and reassures clients of the value and expertise they will receive from the consulting or coaching sessions.

Monitoring the performance of consulting or coaching services involves tracking metrics such as the number of clients, session duration, client satisfaction, testimonials, and client progress or achievements. Creators analyze this data to evaluate the impact and effectiveness of their services, identify areas for improvement, and enhance the overall client experience.

Maintaining professionalism, confidentiality, and ethical standards is essential in providing consulting or coaching services. Creators adhere to ethical guidelines, maintain client confidentiality, and ensure that they offer advice or guidance within their expertise and capabilities.

Creators must strike a balance between promoting their consulting or coaching services and delivering regular content to their broader audience. They aim to offer valuable free content while also providing additional personalized services to those seeking more in-depth guidance and support.

In conclusion, providing consulting or coaching services based on one's expertise offers content creators on platforms like YouTube an opportunity to extend their impact and help individuals seeking personalized guidance and solutions within their niche. By leveraging their knowledge, experience, and skills, creators can offer valuable one-on-one or group consultations, mentoring, or coaching sessions to assist clients in achieving their goals. When executed effectively, consulting or coaching services can serve as an additional revenue stream for creators while positively impacting the lives of their clients by providing them with the necessary guidance and support to succeed in their respective fields.

Chapter- 12

12. **Live Events and Meet-ups:** Organize paid live events, workshops, or meet-ups for your audience.

Organizing paid live events, workshops, or meet-ups for an audience provides content creators on platforms like YouTube with an opportunity to engage with their followers in person, offer exclusive experiences, and create memorable interactions beyond the digital realm. These events serve as a way for creators to connect more intimately with their audience, offer specialized content, and create a sense of community among their followers.

Creators often have dedicated and enthusiastic followers who are eager to engage with them and other like-minded individuals in a real-world setting. Organizing live events, workshops, or meet-ups allows creators to bring their audience together, offering an immersive and interactive experience.

To initiate such events, creators can plan and organize gatherings, workshops, seminars, or meet-ups based on their content niche or audience interests. The events can range from educational workshops, seminars on specific topics, live performances, Q&A sessions, networking opportunities, or social gatherings.

The promotion and marketing of these events play a crucial role in attracting attendees. Creators utilize their existing platforms, such as YouTube channels, social media, email newsletters, and websites, to promote the events. They may create dedicated videos or promotional content, offer early-bird discounts, or conduct giveaways to generate interest and encourage their audience to attend.

Ticketing or registration is often employed for paid events, allowing creators to manage the number of attendees, collect payments, and plan logistics effectively. Creators may partner with event management platforms or use ticketing services to facilitate the registration process and ensure a smooth experience for attendees.

Engagement and interaction during live events are key elements in creating a memorable experience for attendees. Creators aim to engage with their audience, offer valuable content or experiences, and provide opportunities for attendees to interact with each other and the creator, fostering a sense of belonging and community.

Monitoring the success of live events involves tracking metrics such as ticket sales, attendance, participant feedback, social media engagement, and overall satisfaction levels. Creators analyze this data to evaluate the effectiveness of their events, identify areas for improvement, and enhance future event planning.

Ensuring the safety, organization, and professionalism of live events is paramount. Creators prioritize attendee experience by planning logistics, securing appropriate venues, providing necessary facilities, and ensuring a seamless and enjoyable experience for attendees.

Maintaining a balance between organizing live events and creating regular content is crucial. Creators strive to continue delivering high-quality content while also offering exclusive experiences through live events, thereby catering to both online and offline audience engagement.

In conclusion, organizing paid live events, workshops, or meet-ups for an audience presents content creators on platforms like YouTube with an opportunity to extend their impact beyond the digital realm. By bringing their audience together in person, creators can foster a stronger sense of community, offer exclusive experiences, and create lasting memories for their followers. When executed effectively, live events serve as an additional means for creators to engage with their audience, create a closer connection, and provide unique and immersive experiences that complement their online content.

Chapter- 13

13. **Selling Digital Products:** Offer digital downloads such as eBooks, presets, or templates related to your content.

Offering digital products, such as eBooks, presets, templates, or other downloadable content related to a content creator's niche, provides an avenue to monetize expertise, creativity, and specialized knowledge beyond the traditional content available on platforms like YouTube. These digital products offer audiences additional value, insights, or tools related to the creator's content, catering to their specific interests or needs.

Creators often possess expertise, unique techniques, or insights within their niche that may need to be fully explored or explained in their regular content due to time constraints or the need for more comprehensive explanations. Digital products serve as a platform for creators to package and share this specialized knowledge in a more structured and in-depth format.

To initiate the sale of digital products, creators can leverage various platforms or tools designed for digital product distribution, such as Gumroad, Shopify, Etsy, or their websites. These platforms offer creators the necessary infrastructure to create, market, sell, and deliver digital products to their audience.

Creators identify key areas or topics within their niche that align with their expertise and audience interests to develop digital products. These products can include eBooks, guides, tutorials, presets for photo or video editing software, templates for graphics or designs, audio files, or any other content that offers value to their audience.

Promotion and marketing are essential in attracting buyers to these digital products. Creators leverage their existing platforms, such as YouTube channels, social media, email newsletters, and websites, to promote their digital products. They may offer sneak peeks, testimonials, or samples of digital products to generate interest and encourage their audience to make a purchase.

Engagement and interaction with buyers are crucial aspects of selling digital products. Creators aim to provide excellent customer service, engage with buyers for feedback or suggestions, and offer ongoing support related to the digital products purchased.

Creators often showcase the value and benefits of their digital products by highlighting their unique features, practical applications, or testimonials from satisfied buyers. This builds credibility and reassures potential buyers of the value they will receive from purchasing the digital products.

Monitoring the performance of digital product sales involves tracking metrics such as sales volume, revenue generated, customer feedback, download numbers, and overall satisfaction levels. Creators analyze this data to evaluate the effectiveness of their digital products, identify popular products or topics, and refine their future offerings.

Ensuring the quality, relevance, and usefulness of digital products is essential. Creators strive to provide high-quality content that meets the needs and expectations of their audience, thereby fostering customer satisfaction and encouraging repeat purchases.

Maintaining a balance between promoting digital products and creating regular content is crucial. Creators aim to offer valuable free content while also providing additional resources or tools through digital products to those seeking more in-depth knowledge or specialized content.

In conclusion, selling digital products related to a content creator's niche presents an opportunity to extend their impact and provide additional value to their audience beyond the content available on platforms like YouTube. By packaging their expertise, insights, or creative assets into downloadable products, creators can offer a more structured and comprehensive experience to their audience. When executed effectively, selling digital products serves as an additional revenue stream for creators, while providing valuable resources or tools that cater to the specific interests and needs of their audience.

Chapter- 14

14. **Licensing Content:** License your videos or footage to media outlets, agencies, or businesses.

Licensing content, such as videos or footage, to media outlets, agencies, businesses, or other creators, provides content creators on platforms like YouTube with an opportunity to monetize their content beyond the platform itself. This involves granting permission for others to use their original content in exchange for a licensing fee, allowing the content to be utilized in various projects, commercials, documentaries, news segments, or other forms of media.

Creators often produce high-quality, unique, or niche-specific content on their YouTube channels that may be sought after by media outlets, advertising agencies, filmmakers, or businesses looking for specific visuals or storytelling elements to enhance their projects.

To license their content, creators establish terms and agreements outlining the usage rights, duration, territories, and other conditions for the content's use. Creators may negotiate directly with interested parties or collaborate with licensing agencies or platforms that specialize in connecting content creators with potential buyers.

Platforms like Getty Images, Shutterstock, Adobe Stock, or specialized licensing agencies provide creators with the infrastructure to showcase and license their content to a broader audience. These platforms manage the licensing process, handle negotiations, ensure legal compliance, and collect royalties on behalf of creators.

Creators often showcase their licensed content through portfolios or galleries on these platforms, providing potential buyers with access to a diverse range of high-quality visuals or footage available for licensing.

Promotion and marketing of licensed content involve showcasing the value and versatility of the content available for licensing. Creators use their existing platforms, such as YouTube channels, social media, websites, or newsletters, to promote their portfolio of licensable content, highlight the uniqueness or versatility of their visuals, and attract potential buyers.

Engagement and negotiation with interested buyers are crucial aspects of licensing content. Creators aim to establish clear communication, understand the buyer's requirements, negotiate pricing or terms, and provide ongoing support throughout the licensing process.

Monitoring the performance of licensed content involves tracking metrics such as licensing agreements, sales volume, revenue generated, viewer engagement with licensed content, and overall client satisfaction. Creators analyze this data to evaluate the effectiveness of their licensing efforts, identify popular content for licensing, and refine their future offerings.

Maintaining the integrity of the content while licensing is essential. Creators ensure that their content is used appropriately, adhering to the agreed-upon terms and rights granted to the licensee, thus protecting their intellectual property rights.

Balancing the licensing of content with creating regular content for their audience is crucial for creators. They aim to continue producing high-quality content for their YouTube channel while also leveraging their existing content library for licensing opportunities.

In conclusion, licensing content to media outlets, agencies, businesses, or other creators offers content creators on platforms like YouTube an additional revenue stream by monetizing their original content beyond the platform. By showcasing their high-quality visuals or footage for licensing through specialized platforms or agencies, creators can cater to the diverse needs of potential buyers seeking specific visuals or storytelling elements. When executed effectively, content licensing serves as a lucrative opportunity for creators to monetize their content while expanding its reach and usage across various media and commercial projects.

Chapter- 15

15. **Subscription-based Content:** Create a subscription model for exclusive content, behind-the-scenes access, or special features.

Establishing a subscription-based model for exclusive content, behind-the-scenes access, or special features offers content creators on platforms like YouTube a way to provide additional value to their audience while creating a recurring revenue stream. This model allows creators to offer premium content or perks to subscribers in exchange for a subscription fee, fostering a closer connection with their most dedicated followers.

Creators often have loyal and engaged followers who are eager for more personalized or exclusive content that goes beyond what is available for free on their YouTube channel. A subscription-based model allows creators to cater to this demand by offering additional content, exclusive insights, or behind-the-scenes access to their most dedicated audience.

To implement a subscription-based model, creators can utilize platforms or tools specifically designed for membership programs, such as Patreon, YouTube Memberships, or other subscription-based platforms. These platforms provide creators with the infrastructure to set up different membership tiers, offer exclusive perks, and manage the subscription process.

Creators develop membership tiers that offer varying levels of access or perks based on the subscription fee. These perks may include exclusive videos, live streams, behind-the-scenes content, early access to videos, members-only Q&A sessions, exclusive merchandise, shoutouts, or direct interaction with the creator.

Promotion and marketing of subscription-based content involve highlighting the value and benefits of membership tiers to potential subscribers. Creators leverage their existing platforms, such as YouTube channels, social media, websites, or newsletters, to promote their subscription-based content, enticing their audience with sneak peeks or teasers of the exclusive content and perks available to subscribers.

Engagement and interaction with subscribers are key aspects of a successful subscription-based model. Creators aim to foster a sense of community among their subscribers, providing personalized attention, responding to messages or comments, and offering exclusive content that aligns with their subscribers' interests.

Monitoring the performance of subscription-based content involves tracking metrics such as subscriber growth, retention rates, engagement levels, feedback from subscribers, and overall satisfaction with the membership program. Creators analyze this data to evaluate the effectiveness of their subscription tiers, identify popular perks, and refine their membership offerings to better meet their audience's needs.

Maintaining the balance between offering exclusive subscription-based content and creating regular free content is crucial for creators. They aim to continue providing high-quality content to their broader audience while offering additional perks and exclusive content to their subscribers.

In conclusion, implementing a subscription-based model for exclusive content, behind-the-scenes access, or special features provides content creators on platforms like YouTube an opportunity to engage more intimately with their audience and create a sustainable revenue stream. By offering premium content or perks to dedicated subscribers, creators can foster a closer connection with their audience, offer additional value, and create a sense of exclusivity for their most committed followers. When executed effectively, subscription-based content models serve as a valuable way for creators to monetize their content while providing tailored experiences and benefits to their most loyal audience members.

www.ingramcontent.com/pod-product-compliance
Lightning Source LLC
LaVergne TN
LVHW072051060326
832903LV00054B/400